THE ART OF
RESPONSIBILITY

freedom to create your own life

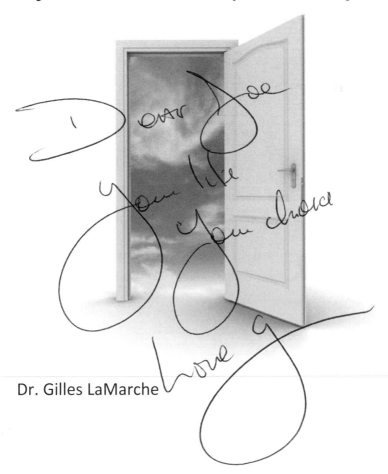

Dr. Gilles LaMarche

It's **your** life.

YOU

are responsible

for **your** results.

It's time to turn up the heat. Will you?

Copyright © 2012

Published in the United States by

Insight Publishing

707 West Main Street, Suite 5
Sevierville, TN 37862
800-989-7771
www.insightpublishing.com

ISBN - 978-1-60013-806-5

10 9 8 7 6 5 4 3 2 1

Table of Contents

Acknowledgments

When your "why" is strong enough, the how usually shows up, and along the way you encounter people who inspire you to be a better version of yourself than you ever thought possible.

To my dear and beautiful children Dr. Jason Paul Lamarche, Alanna Lizanne Clark, and Christopher Marc Lamarche, you continue to inspire me to give of myself and serve to my greatest ability. Thank you for allowing me this freedom. I am very proud of the fabulous adults you have become, and of the partners you have attracted into your lives. I love you dearly. To Jason's wife Dr. Rebecca Lamarche, thank you for loving my son as you do and for being an inspiration to him. To Michael Adrian Clark, Alanna's husband, thank you for being the kind and gentle soul that you are, and for loving Alanna as you do. To Christopher's special lady and soon to be wife, Melissa Green, thank you for the joy you bring to Christopher's heart. I so enjoy watching how he looks at you when you walk into a room.

You, children, are my "why".

To my mother, Therese Lamarche, thank you for sharing your perseverance and courage of what is possible. You are my hero.

To my three sisters, Susan Lamarche, Lizanne Gonzales, and Sylvie Lamarche-Lacroix, thank you for being who you are.

To Dre. Renée Dallaire, and her children Camille and Pascal, thank you for the contributions you have made to my life. I am eternally grateful.

To my many mentors who breathed life into my career, who believed in me and offered guidance, thank you for taking me seriously. Your devotion to your "why" inspired me to discover mine.

To the business partners and team members that have shared time and expertise with me in the past 30 years, thank you for your support and contributions.

To our present team at Parker University, in Dallas, TX, including President Dr. Fabrizio Mancini and the Executive Team, Administration, Faculty and Students, The Board of Trustees under the chairmanship of Mr. Bill Nardiello, my Executive Assistant Ms Sharon Zamora and all those I get the pleasure to work with everyday, thank you for being members of an "A" team that is directed to understanding and living it's "why".

To those many supporters who have given me wings (you are many and you know who you are); from my home town of Timmins, Ontario, to those I had the pleasure to serve with at The College of Chiropractors of Ontario in Toronto, Canada; to the thousands of patients I was honored to serve; to clients from around the world who entrusted me as their coach, thank you for believing in me and for allowing me to serve you.

To two special friends who always have something great to tell me, who inspire me to be all that I can be, Dr. Bharat Jasani and Dr. Stacey Olson; words alone cannot express the gratitude I feel for you.

And to all who have shared their wisdom, humor and genius, you have allowed me to see the grand scheme of this world. I would not be the same without your influence.

A note from Dr. Gilles LaMarche

Responsibility is a word and a life theme that I have kept close to my heart for decades. I often wonder where this all began. In retrospect I can see this theme developing from a very young age. I started working for my father in his small grocery store at the age of six. The tasks were simple, yet putting cans on a shelf or pounds of butter in a cooler in an orderly manner required attention. My father described that all the items needed to neatly face the clients as they looked for product, and this was essential to creating a great business. A few years later this theme of excellence was highlighted by Mr. Sirocco who ran the local newspaper delivery service. He instructed his young paper boys to treat every client with respect, to be aware of their needs, what door they preferred to receive their newspaper and how early they preferred to receive it. He made us aware that customer service was primary to running our independent paper routes, and I thrived with more than 100 clients receiving the Toronto Star six days per week. Every week my income rose because of the consistent tips I received for excellent service. I was taking responsibility on my service delivery promise to the clients and they were rewarding me. My father later became a travelling salesman so I was given increased home responsibilities. Yet I had become accustomed to my own income, saved my 10% as instructed, enjoyed being somewhat financially independent, and took on extra work cutting lawns in the summer, and shoveling snow in the winter. My newspaper clients knew that I was a responsible young man, so it was easy to get extra work, and all this before age 10. My sense of responsibility seemed innate. Responsible was who I was. I excelled in my studies skipping two grades in elementary school, and found myself in 9th grade by the age of 12. My birthday is in February, so I was quite young to be entering high school, let alone an all boys catholic school. That same year I met Mr. Eddie Vaillancourt, a well to do local business man, a man of deep principle who further instilled the value of responsibility, courage, perseverance and service in business. He was a man of his word, a man who lived by honesty and integrity, an example for me to aspire to. These same values were being shared with me by my mother who survived a series of health challenges, yet always remained steadfast in her ability to be a caring and loving mother. To this day her courage inspires me, and I would have to say that she is my number one hero. This theme has continued to evolve throughout my life, and most who know me would tell you that I always take my responsibilities seriously. I had the honor to graduate from the University of Toronto, and four years later from the Canadian Memorial Chiropractic College. On my scholastic journey I had the privilege to meet countless individuals who had a major impact on me, people who truly lived The ART of Responsibility, people who lived by example. I thank all of them for their contributions to my life. As a practicing Doctor of Chiropractic, this ART became a significant tool allowing me to serve my patients with ease and love, something reinforced by Dr. James W. Parker, my chiropractic mentor.

A few years later God blessed me with three wonderful children, and it is so rewarding to see that they too have embraced this theme for their lives.

People who choose to be responsible take psychological ownership for what they say they will do. They do what others are not willing to do, and therefore achieve results others can only begin to imagine achieving.

The ART of Responsibility – *freedom to create your own life* is written to help you do exactly that, create your own life filled with value, and decide how you will impact the lives of others universally by choosing to tap into your talents and share them with the world responsibly. Welcome to this journey of discovery and possibility.

Introduction –

Understanding the power of taking responsibility

"Though no one can go back and make a brand new start, anyone can start from now and make a brand new ending."

- Carl Bard

Taking full responsibility for your life experiences is not always easy, until you experience the almost magical quality you will feel when you do. I assume that since you have this book in your hands right now, you are looking to improve some condition of "YOU". The first relationship you have is with yourself. This relationship sets the tone for all other relationships. You teach people how to treat you by how you choose to treat yourself. Focus starting today, on discovering and appreciating your own goodness. Focus on loving yourself the way you ultimately want others to love you. Then you can move to looking at others. Whatever your position or lot in life, you will always be given an opportunity to make a difference in someone else's, if you choose to. I ask you to watch for the signs. Guaranteed, signs are all around you. Become aware of your true purpose and how you can serve a fellow human being. As a start, focus on taking one action that will make someone's day. What you will discover as a result is a transformation in your own life.

Choose one relationship in your life that needs healing. Forgive this person for what they have done or failed to do. Look for the good in them, and then take the time to share it whether on paper, on the telephone or face to face. Say a prayer for them or send them goodwill wishes. Be grateful for what the Universe is teaching you through them.

Choose to be happy today. Everything you have thus far is by choice, including happiness. You can choose how you feel. You can choose what you love, who you love, and how you love.

"No one can make you happy if you choose to be unhappy, and no one can make you unhappy if you choose to be happy."

- Paramahansa Yogananda

Regularly repeat "Something wonderful is going to happen today." By doing so you are setting yourself up for success. You are taking responsibility for your thoughts.

"To be who you have never been and get what you have never had, YOU must become who you have never been and do what you've never done."

- Gilles LaMarche

"You are responsible, forever, for what you have tamed. You are responsible for your rose."

- Antoine de Saint-Exupery

Chapter One

Accepting Personal Responsibility

They say that the quality of the answer always depends on the quality of the question. In this chapter we consider some empowering questions and provide guidance that will allow you the opportunity to step into a wonderful world created through The ART of Responsibility.

What is self discipline and what is really meant by the term "accepting personal responsibility"?

When you fail to accept personal responsibility, what consequences are you likely to live or not live?

When you choose to accept personal responsibility, how different might your life be?

What are the beliefs of those individuals who have not yet accepted personal responsibility for their life?

What are the beliefs of those who accept personal responsibility?

If you choose to accept personal responsibility, what behavior traits must you develop and own?

"You can choose the pain of discipline or the pain of regret. The choice is yours."

Gilles LaMarche

"It is not only what we do, but also what we do not do, for which we are accountable."

Molière

Most of you hold several roles, functions and responsibilities; you are a child, possibly also a parent, a friend, and maybe a spouse; you are likely an employee or an employer, or a self employed professional, a consumer, a citizen, a contributor to society. Somewhere along the way you are likely to face some type of road block. Your character may be challenged; your emotions sent askew, your physical and mental prowess tested. Personal responsibility is your ability to take care of yourself by means of, keeping healthy, managing your emotions, keeping a sound mind, treating yourself with respect, taking responsibility for your actions, accepting the consequences that come from those actions and understanding that what you do impacts you and everyone around you. As a responsible individual you have the capacity to determine what's right or wrong, what's good or bad, what's within or outside your control. If you take personal responsibility you are likely to move in the direction you aspire living. If you are not taking personal responsibility, you likely have the inclination to put the blame on your lack of personal growth and success on everyone else but yourself. If you are consistently looking to blame others for your lot in life, and you are unwilling to look at the person that stares you in the mirror (YOU), you will not advance in life. It becomes imperative that you change your focus. In this instance the solution is to seek to forgive so you can change your focus. It matters not what has occurred in the past, or who may have done you wrong; it only matters that you make a concerted effort to focus your energy on today, since this will determine how you live your future. Ask yourself these questions: "How can failing to make a change negatively impact me and my future?" "How will making a change positively impact my future?" Personal responsibility is an obligation to you. It is your willingness to ensure your good character and behavior irrespective of your past. Individual responsibility includes being accountable for your health, wealth, success and happiness. If you are living in a mess and find yourself in a disorderly life, recognize that you somehow allowed that to be created. Life always gives you consequences related to your actions or your inaction. What if you chose to see responsibility as a blessing rather than a burden; could that change your focus? In his article Personal Responsibility, Chuck Gallozzi sates: "When we take responsibility, we admit we are the ones responsible for the choices we make. We, not other people or events, are responsible for the way we think and feel. It is our life, and we are in charge of it. We are free to enjoy it or disdain it. No, we're not responsible for all that happens to us, but we are responsible for how we think, feel and act when they happen."

Accepting responsibility includes a variety of issues. Yes it requires that you acknowledge that you are solely responsible for the choices you make in your life, that only you can choose to feel or think the way you do. When accepting responsibility you do not blame others for the choices you've made. You tear down the mask of defense for why you may have thought others responsible for who you have become or for what you're bound to become. By choosing personal responsibility you come to realize that you determine your feelings about any event or action addressed to you, no matter how negative this may appear. You become your best cheerleader by choosing to become the best version of you. It has never been and will never be in your best interest to solely depend on others to make you feel good about you. You can choose to take hold of your life, give it direction and reason, by taking preventive health enhancing steps to structure your life so that you will achieve the outcome that you set for yourself. In the next chapter I will ask you to take an honest inventory of your strengths, abilities, talents, and positive aspects of your character and your life. This will help you develop positive self-affirming statements to enhance your personal development and overall life experience. If you are holding blame or anger towards anyone that you believe has caused you wrong, recognize that they always did the best they could, given the limitations of their life experience, background, knowledge or awareness. Choosing to hold on to this anger or blame limits your growth. Choosing forgiveness will enhance your life and the life of everyone you come in contact with in the future.

You may have asked yourself, "Why is taking personal responsibility for my life so important, and how can failing to make a change towards responsibility create negative consequences?" It has been discovered that those who fail to accept personal responsibility often run the risk of becoming overly dependent on acceptance, approval, and affirmation from others. When you expect recognition from others and don't receive it, you are likely to become overwhelmed by disabling fears, making you unable to discover your true strengths and talents. This type of thinking will keep you from taking even a small risk or from making even a minor decision. This leads to difficulties in relationships both professional and personal, and often causes an individual to search for recognition or pleasure through abuse of alcohol or recreational drugs, excessive eating or gambling, excessive shopping, sex or work. Living a life of excesses typically occurs with people who fail to take full responsibility for themselves. Failing to take personal responsibility does result in negative consequences.

People who do not accept personal responsibility often are heard using words such as: "It's not my fault that I'm the way I am. Look at my parents." They also talk about never asking to be born; they see little value in their life, see life as unfair and wonder why they should bother going on. You hear them use language such as "Life isn't fair. There's no sense in trying to take control of my life. Nobody really cares. I'm useless, I'm a failure." They think that they've been given an unlucky break, and fail to recognize that luck comes to those who prepare and seize the opportunity when it is presented. They ask the questions - "How can I possibly be responsible for what happens to me? Don't you understand that there is such thing as fate, wicked and jealous people, and all sorts of negative influences that have a greater bearing on my future than I do?" They blame their present situation on others, racism, bigotry, prejudice, sexism, their age, the town where they were born, the economy, their friends or lack thereof. You often hear them say: "I am who I am. I just can't change." These are the people who choose to live a life of martyrdom, self-pity, blame others and resist help. Unfortunately, their chronic anger usually leads to depression, mental instability, aggressive and hostile behavior, and a deep seated belief that they are unable and unworthy.

Accepting personal responsibility requires the development and use of certain traits. It all begins with self-acceptance, and a reverence for the fact that you were born and made great. Anger, fear, blame, mistrust and insecurity, must be replaced by forgiveness, gratitude and unconditional love. The willingness to be open to new ideas or concepts about life and the human condition will set you on the path to reorganize your priorities. You will realize that you are the one in charge of the direction of your life from now on, and that you have the capacity to choose your responses to everyone in your life, and to everything that happens to you from this point forward.

On the website www.livestrong.com I discovered a section that deals with steps in accepting personal responsibility. I share these with you not quite verbatim, but in a fashion that I believe to be user friendly.

Step 1: To decide if you are having problems accepting personal responsibility, answer the following questions in your journal:

a) How frequently do you allow others to determine who you are today?

b) How easy is it to accept that you are responsible for your choices in life?

c) How easy is it for you to believe that you determine the direction your life takes?

d) How easy is it for you to blame others for where you are today?

e) How frequently do you feel sorry for yourself?

f) What masks do you hide behind to avoid accepting personal responsibility?

g) How rational are you in dealing with the part you played in being who you are today?

h) How easy is it for you to accept blame or admit mistakes?

i) How easy is it for you to accept that you determine your feelings when negative events occur in your life?

j) How easy is it for you to depend solely on yourself, for acceptance, affirmation and approval?

k) How willing are you to be the sole determinant for the health of your self- esteem?

l) How easy is it for you to let go of guilt if you stop rescuing those in your life?

m) How willingly do you take preventive steps to ensure your physical, spiritual and emotional well-being?

n) How successfully do you practice gratitude and forgiveness in order to get on with your life?

o) How successfully have you practiced self-affirmation in your life?

Step 2: Rate yourself on a scale of 1 to 5 as to the level of personal responsibility you have accepted in each of the following areas: (see scale below)

Rating Area in your life:

a) I take preventive and maintenance measures to ensure my physical health ___

b) I take preventive and maintenance measures to ensure my emotional health ___

c) I take preventive and maintenance measures to ensure my spiritual health ___

d) I choose to eat quality food and drink plenty of water to enhance my well-being ___

e) I choose to maintain my optimum healthy weight ___

f) I avoid smoking, excessive drinking and drug abuse ___

g) I avoid excessive gambling, shopping and disparaging behavior ___

h) I control my work environment and choose work/life balance ___
i) I take preventive and maintenance measures to ensure healthy relationships ___
j) I take the necessary steps to overcome problems/difficulties ___
k) I take necessary steps to protect myself from being victimized by my rescuing and enabling of others ___
l) I manage my time, the stress in my life, and choose to overcome my fears ___

SCALE

1. = always irresponsible
2. = usually irresponsible
3. = irresponsibility balanced out with responsibility (neutral)
4. = usually responsible
5. = always responsible

SCORE – A rating of 3 or less in any of the areas indicates a need to create a plan towards accepting personal responsibility. A rating of 4 or 5 tells you that you have chosen to take control of your decision making process, and the outcomes you enjoy. Congratulations.

STEP 3: If you scored 3 or below in any area, take time to identify your beliefs that prevent acceptance of responsibility for yourself. Once these have been identified, develop rational replacement beliefs that will lead you to accept responsibility for yourself.

Example

Limiting belief: *"I'm useless at love because my parents were divorced."*

Replacement Belief: *"I choose to be unconditionally loving of myself, knowing that how I behave allows me to attract love into my life."*

Beliefs that prevent you from accepting responsibility

_____

_____

_____

_____

_____

_____

_____

_____

_____

_____

_____

_____

_____

Replacement beliefs to accept personal responsibility

_____

_____

_____

_____

_____

_____

_____

_____

_____

_____

Take these exercises seriously and follow through. You will be on your way to discovering "freedom to create your own life".

We are going to assume that you've chosen to follow through and are committed to your progress. Once you make a solid agreement with yourself, you will begin to notice whenever an agreement has been broken. For example, if you make an agreement with your spouse to stop by the grocery store and pick up certain items and you forget to do so, it is imperative that you silently note that you have broken this agreement. You have created a small bump in what could have been a completely smooth road. You can now choose to do what it takes to correct the situation. When you set your intention to be 100% responsible for your agreements, you experience the harmony when you follow through, and the obvious disharmony that you create in your universe when you fail to be fully responsible.

Take Action Now

Focus on a simple agreement that you make often, maybe even daily. What is this agreement?

_____

_____

_____

AFFIRMATION for GROWTH – *I keep my agreements.*

- Make a conscious effort to do exactly what you said you would do, at the exact time you said it would be done.
- If you sense that you may not meet the agreement, immediately contact the person with whom you made the agreement and renegotiate something that is acceptable to them. This is truly about living up to your agreement made with the other individual.
- It is important that you allow for the unexpected. For example if your agreement was to show up on time, be aware of your environment and the possibility that traffic may delay you. Look at your gas gauge in advance to make sure that you will have plenty of fuel to get there.
- Ask yourself questions pertinent to your commitment such as: "Do I have my wallet; am I dressed appropriately for the occasion; do I know exactly how to get to where I am going; do I have the ingredients to make the dinner I promised I would make?"
- "Be prepared" is the motto for keeping your promises.

"Triumph often is nearest when defeat seems inescapable."

B.C.Forbes (Forbes Magazine founder)

Chapter Two

Personal Responsibility –
Finding your source of inspiration

Do you have what it takes to choose greatness? I hope you answered yes, because you do have what it takes to choose greatness for your life and the lives of those you love. Past performance does not equal present or future potential. Everyone can choose, starting today, to live by higher standards, and take greater responsibility for their outcomes. We have all heard the saying "If it is to be, it's up to me." This is not only lip service, it is fact. People who choose to live a responsible life are held in high regard because of their dependability and consistent values. They are individuals that others can rely on. Why? Because they do what they said they would do, and they are impelled to deliver on their commitments, and meet their obligations. This is the reason why we view responsible individuals as trustworthy and dependable. When pressed to complete a task they draw on their reserves of personal accountability. Fulfilling commitments spurs them to do whatever it takes to complete projects or deliver on a promise, and they do it with honesty and integrity. Their word is their bond.

For others it seems easier to defend actions than to honestly examine themselves and their behaviors. They are quicker to attack than to admit fault or defeat. You know that admission requires courage. When you summon and embrace the courage to take ownership of your past and present moment experiences, to see the experiences as they are, to get a sense of this reality and truly feel the experiences, you get a better sense of your life path. The blueprint of your life becomes so much clearer. With clarity you have a capacity to face your fears and discover the beliefs that create these fears. Fear has derailed more people from their purpose, from living the life they want, than almost any hurdle we know of. Fear is experienced by many as a self imposed prison. It affects every part of your life – relationships, family, career, physical and spiritual health, you name it, and fear affects it. To defeat fear, you must reject comfort and embrace growth. Comfort comes as a guest, stays to host us, and enslaves us to the rest of our lives. Yes, you must reject comfort when necessary and be careful not to fear pain and suffering. All growth and everything you desire reside just outside of your comfort zones. You must embrace feeling uncomfortable, willing to take a chance in faith. To fully defeat fear you must create a massive crystal clear vision for your life, understand what will make it count, and make a difference for you and others. Fear prevents you from thinking big and setting massive goals for your life. Once you have a vision and clear goals, steps on how you will move forward, the excitement and energy you receive become the driving force for your life. This force is truly contagious. A crystal clear vision shared often inspires others to want to get on board, assist in any way they can, and forces you to keep moving when times get difficult. It is never, "Will times get tough?" It's more about "When times get tough…" You either attract others to assist you, or you force yourself to grow and increase your competencies. Either way you win, and who you become in the process can never be taken away from you. This is your experience, your life.

An acronym that I have learned to appreciate is FEAR - False Evidence Appearing Real. Anyone who has ever feared, can tell you how real the fear is; how it plays a negative role in their life; how it affects their sleep, their work, their relationships, and their overall health and wellbeing. At the same time anyone who has ever overcome a fear can tell you that in retrospect the fear they faced for years truly was false evidence appearing real at the time.

"Responsibility is the thing people dread most of all. Yet it is the one thing in the world that develops us, gives us manhood or womanhood fiber."

Frank Crane

"If you don't run your own life, someone else will." These are words that spoke to me very loudly when I first heard those decades ago, and I believe that it is at that moment that I chose to direct my own life and take greater responsibility for my choices. Your power of choice is always available and waiting for you. It does not guarantee immunity from the trials of life, since there will always be a series of ups and downs as you travel your journey. The power of choice extends an invitation to all who use this tremendous gift to humanity as an instrument of grace. This is an invitation to a future of freedom, happiness and truth that is meant to be real for every human being on this wonderful planet. The doorway to authentic love, truth, joy, freedom and peace that your power of choice opens up, leads to experience a life of connectedness like no other. *"It is in the moment of decision that you shape your destiny."* All that you are right now is the result of how you have thought in the past. Past performance does not equal present potential. I invite you to see your life as your canvas and you as the artist. When you realize that nothing changes until you take full responsibility for your thoughts and your actions, you begin to understand that change cannot be a "should" or" hope to". For real change to occur, you must. I can hear some of you saying "it can't be that simple a process." Well, you don't know until you take a new approach to your life, and if you miss, change your approach again. All that you need to achieve what you desire is already in you, and it begins by developing a heightened level of awareness for what you are thinking now. If the thoughts you have serve you and lead you closer to living the life that you aspire, keep thinking that way; if not, it's time to change the way you think. Most people have difficulty separating themselves from their thoughts. It is imperative to realize that you are not your thoughts. Yes you have thoughts that lead you to take the actions you take, but your thoughts do not define who you are. You can choose to listen to the thoughts you have, or choose better

thoughts when realizing that certain thoughts really do not serve you or others. Negative self talk is usually devastating, and pulls you in directions that you really don't want to go in; but most people listen to their thoughts no matter what. Let's make it real for a moment. Is there something you have been telling yourself that you will do, maybe for weeks or months, and you have not yet started? What might that be? Take a moment to think about these issues and write them down right here.

_____

_____

_____

_____

_____

_____

_____

_____

_____

Do you have thoughts that support you taking action, yet other thoughts that sabotage your efforts to move forward? Are you aware of these thought processes? If not, recognize that you could choose to develop a greater awareness for the thoughts that drive you. By being more aware you can differentiate between the thoughts that guide you towards the life you aspire living and the thoughts that pull you away. It requires that you truly pay attention to how you think, and at pivotal moments change a sabotaging thought for a more inspiring thought. You have the power to choose the thoughts that serve you best. Many people live their life as if they had no real choices, sometimes completely by ignorance. A choice is only a choice when you know without a doubt that you have a choice, and take responsibility for what you allow to direct your life. The thoughts people have are often inaccurate, negative, harmful or even destructive, and usually created by past experiences. Choosing such thoughts can sabotage your efforts to make good balanced decisions. When you recognize that certain thoughts will not serve you, metaphorically step back, listen intently, then make choices that are most aligned with who you choose to become. You have a choice to think differently, and this requires that you be fully responsible. That's why we say that success is a conscious choice. Throughout your life there will be critical moments when your success or failure will be determined by the choices you will make in the moment. This is what we call pivotal moments. Learning to recognize these moments and making better choices is the key to creating a successful life. After all, you do want to be in control of your life don't you?

How often have you tried to convince yourself or people around you that everything in your life is fabulous, even when you know that some areas in your life are far from satisfying? Choosing to live a successful life requires a very high degree of self honesty, introspection, a willingness to take inventory of where you have been and where you want to go. You must therefore explore the thoughts that drive your feelings, emotions, actions, behaviors, and ultimately the results you are creating and experiencing in your life. Take time to make it real and write down the thoughts that have been driving you. This is definitely worth the effort.

_____

_____

_____

_____

_____

_____

_____

_____

_____

_____

_____

_____

_____

_____

_____

_____

Are you ready to make better conscious choices to create the life that you aspire living? Hopefully you answered a clear and loud "YES".

Living in the Now and taking full responsibility for your thoughts, choices and actions will lead you to do what is necessary to turn your dreams into reality. Living in the Now is the only place where you can function clearly, or learn to function clearly.

> *"If you are depressed, you are living in the past.*
> *If you are anxious, you are living in the future.*
> *If you are at peace, you are living in the present."*
>
> (Lao Tzu)

If you are not living in the Now and taking focused directed action to achieve the life that you aspire living, where are you?

_____

_____

_____

_____

_____

You don't actually want to stay there do you? Take a few moments to write down what you want to achieve in the next 6-8 weeks, and who you want to become in the process. This is the first step to taking responsibility for your outcomes, for your life.

_____
_____
_____
_____
_____
_____
_____
_____
_____
_____
_____
_____
_____
_____
_____
_____
_____
_____

Later you can take the time to create a one year plan, as well as 5 and 10 year plans. May I suggest that you purchase a journal and start writing what you want to attract to your life; the person you will become so that as a natural outcome you would attract your ultimate life to you.

If you are not yet convinced of the value of such exercises, ask yourself this question: "What happens to the present when I am spending valuable time wishing I could change the past?"

_____

_____

_____

_____

_____

Most of us have had thoughts that we would prefer not having. These thoughts can leave us somewhat embarrassed, frustrated, create a sense of anxiety, shame, or guilt. You know without a doubt that such thoughts do not serve you, yet allow them to take control, and self destructive behaviors take over. When you are fully engaged in living in the Now, deeply committed to making wise choices, you will be better positioned to hear your thoughts. You will have a heightened awareness for your first thought, and at pivotal moments will recognize that you have the opportunity to choose to go with what you are thinking, or consciously choose a better second thought. The question that you will learn to ask yourself often is: "Is this thought adding value to my life and moving me closer to my objectives, or will this thought sabotage my efforts to move in the direction of my dreams?" If the thought is likely to sabotage your efforts, choose a better second thought. You must walk where failures fear to walk, work when failures seek to rest. A wonderful affirmation comes from Scroll # IV in the book The Greatest Salesman in the World by Og Mandino.

"I will concentrate my energy on the challenge of the moment and my actions will help me forget all else."

Og Mandino

Dr. James W. Parker wrote a series of life principles he coined The Parker Principles. The one fitting for this discussion is: "<u>Thought + Action = Feeling</u> and it is your feelings that attract your life to you". If you are unhappy with the feelings you are experiencing most of the time, you must increase your responsibility for your thoughts and actions. By choosing thoughts in line with the life you want to experience and acting accordingly, you will get to live the feelings you want to live most of the time.

"My dreams are worthless, my plans are dust, my goals are impossible. All are of no value unless they are followed by action."

Og Mandino

You hear it all the time, the clatter and clang of those trembling and trepid souls who regularly remind you "it can't be done" and "no one has ever done it this way", and surely "we've never done it this way". But you know this to be true don't you – that no great plan and no great life is accomplished without overcoming endless obstacles which test the mettle of your determination and the endurance of what you truly believe? The world seeks those who have a powerful purpose; people who are willing to commit, who sometimes take unconventional positions, who give heart and spirit to the fear, the terror, the surprise and the exhilaration of the unexplored. That's where the rubber meets the road. This is where you see individuals overcoming challenges large and small, the makings of what many would call a hero. Courage and responsibility for the outcome of their life is what makes anyone a hero. Will you be a hero in your life, one who takes charge of your thoughts and actions, and one who listens to God's direction, the direction set for you by Universal Intelligence? You have been given wonderful gifts and talents. It is now time to recognize and use these gifts. Please take time right now to identify your gifts and attributes.

_____

_____

_____

_____

_____

_____

_____

_____

_____

_____

_____

_____

_____

_____

_____

_____

_____

_____

_____

_____

_____

_____

"If you're not inspired to get up in the morning to fulfill your direction, and if you are not enthusiastically working on it, nor doing something you love to do and want to accomplish, people can pick that up. You can't delegate enthusiasm away from you; you have to start with enthusiasm within you."

Dr. John Demartini

Why is having a powerful purpose for your life so crucial to living an extraordinary life? Because purpose inspires you, and when you are inspired by some great purpose:

- Your thoughts transcend their bonds
- Your mind transcends limitations
- Your consciousness expands in every direction
- You find yourself in a new, great and wonderful world
- Dormant forces, faculties and talents come alive
- You discover yourself to be a greater person by far than you ever dreamed possible

Rumi

You may ask, "How does one know she/he is on purpose? How does one find purpose?" Purpose resides in the strength of your "WHY?" Most people describe who they are and what they do from the position of "what". Imagine how your life could be different if you changed your communication to describe who you are and what you do from the position of "why"? When your "why" is strong, you discover the "how" with greater ease and you succeed in accomplishing "what" you want to accomplish. The "why" is always based on service. One of the best renditions of the importance of choosing your "why" comes from Simon Sinek's recorded TED Talk found at the web site below.

www.ted.com/talks/simon_sinek_how_great_leaders_inspire_action

Another great Parker Principle that I have chosen to live from is "Loving service – my first technique". This principle truly is about the "why", yet provides the "how" and the "what" all in one. If you choose to come to life from a position of unconditional love (why you do what you do) and serve humanity to the best of your ability by delivering your service, product or idea from this "special place", your "why" will be felt. You will discover your "how" and others will clearly see your "what". All this requires that you take concerted responsibility for every part of your life; from "why" you think, say and do what you think, say and do; to "how" you think, say and do "what" you think, say and do. Please don't let this confuse you. Just read it again until it sinks in. This is the answer to a greater life.

"I think the purpose of life is to be useful, responsible, honorable, and compassionate. It is, above all, to matter: to count, to stand for something, you have made some difference that you have lived of all."

Leo Rosten

"Life is a gift, and it offers us the privilege, opportunity, and responsibility to give something back by becoming more."

Anthony Robbins

Take Action Now

AFFIRMATION for GROWTH – *I take full and complete responsibility for my experiences.*

- Write down a recent experience that made you feel out of control.
- What negative emotion(s) or feelings were you experiencing?
- What were you thinking while experiencing these negative emotions? Where was your mind exactly? What was that little voice inside your head really saying?
- Imagine this entire scenario as if you were watching a movie on a huge screen.
- Since you are the writer, director and producer, as well as actor in the movie of your life, rewrite the script of that event and choose an improved response. Since we recognize that Thought + Action= Feelings, what thought could you have chosen that would have created a completely different experience?
- You know that you control the thoughts that you allow to permeate your mind. Utilizing a heightened level of awareness, practice choosing your thoughts as your movie unfolds rather than having to come back and create a shift.

Most people live their life as if robot like. However when you choose to be responsible to create your experiences you will discover a sense of personal power and growth. More importantly you will discover a freedom to truly live the life that you aspire living. Take responsibility for creating the experience you want to have, as you add good thoughts and produce great feelings for your life.

Chapter Three

Taking Responsibility for Your Health

Efficiency, as the business guru Peter Drucker once said, is doing things right; effectiveness is doing the right things. Doing the wrong things, as it relates to your health, in an efficient way can cost you dearly. When you look closely at any given day of your life, you realize you might be doing some fun things, and might be doing the easy things. Are you sure, though, that you are doing the right things to live a healthy well balanced life? Years ago I had a discussion with a mentor I truly respected and asked him these questions: "What makes you successful? What do you do to maintain your health and vitality? How do you manage your stress?" His answer to those three questions was very simple: "Do the right things consistently, and do them with a commitment to excellence." I remember those words as if they were uttered to me just yesterday. Furthermore every successful person I've ever had this discussion with gave me a similar answer. You're like every other human being, accountable for doing the right things consistently in your life. If something's not working at the level of excellence that you want, that fact is your responsibility and no one else's. No one else can do your right things for you. And no one else can ensure that you are doing them to the level of excellence that will produce the results you want to achieve. There are two important questions to ask yourself regularly as it relates to situations and conditions that would produce the results that you want for your overall health and well-being.

"If my life depended on the next action I took, how differently would I perform that action?" because doing the wrong thing can have massive consequences.

"What can I do consistently, with a commitment to excellence, that will make it easier to achieve my health goal sooner, rather than later?"

Many people have told me "It's not easy to answer those questions." They have asked; "What can I actually do? What happens if I don't know what my "right things" really are?" My answer to them is quite simple; look at what others are doing to achieve the results that are similar to what you would like to achieve, and take action. This can be a great reality check. Furthermore, choose to interview individuals whether face-to-face or by telephone and ask them the simple question that I asked my mentor decades ago: "What are you doing to stay healthy and vibrant?" You'll be surprised that most people that are truly thriving will give you very similar answers to that question. Once you know what to do, it is imperative that you do this consistently. Yes, it will take courage and discipline, and discipline may be painful. You can choose the pain of discipline or the pain of regret. The choice is yours. The change required is to be greater than your internal voices that talk you away from your own decisions, your own greatness. You will live in either survival or creation. The survival process leads to stress which later knocks you out of coherence. No organism in nature is designed for long-term stress. Stress chemicals emitted by the body are highly addictive and human beings have a tendency to associate issues with emotional addiction. When you live by emotions of stress you will become disconnected from possibility of achieving a more fulfilling life. To create something new you must be willing to think differently, you must be willing to become something else. This is a conscious decision. Most people wait for crisis to get about the business of change. Why wait for a crisis? Why not rise with choice of being inspired and take actions to be fully alive. Aristotle said: "we are what we repeatedly do; therefore excellence is not an act but a habit." Why should you choose to take your health seriously immediately? Because you matter, and those that love you are counting on you to make wise decisions about your health.

"Without self-discipline, success is impossible, period."

Lou Holtz

Throughout the history of mankind, we have searched for methods to improve health and vitality, to make things easier on everyone, to travel faster, to diminish our workload, to increase our standard of living and quality of life. In doing so technological advancements have been created. In an attempt to better understand and heal the human body, many drugs and therapies have been created causing at times more damage than good. An excellent emergency care system has been developed helping millions of people in times of crisis; however we have failed terribly with healthcare.

Many people will tell you that the most precious gift in life is your health. Just ask anyone whose health is failing what they want most of all and they will tell you without hesitation, "my health". You have probably experienced the feeling many times yourself: how great you feel after recovery from a severe cold or after a minor injury is healed. Good health is something healthy people take for granted and something sick people always hope for. Have you ever stopped for a moment to ask yourself why people get sick? Why, for example, does an individual live the first four or five decades of his or her life appearing completely healthy and all of a sudden may die of a massive heart attack? Why does a virus or a bacterium create sniffles in one child and a serious disease in a sibling? Is it not logical to assume that if an individual is born completely normal with all systems functioning to the optimum, that this individual is healthy and should in fact live a long and healthy life? Science today tells us that the human body is created to last 120 to 150 years. Why then is this not the case? It has become apparent that even the nations of Canada and the United States of America, where more money per capita is spent on healthcare and where the greatest resources of scientific minds and technology are found, are also, according to the World Health Organization of the United Nations, statistically some of the unhealthier countries of the developed world; Canada being ranked 37th and the United States being ranked 39th.

Society has come to recognize health as being the absence of symptoms and disease. Due to the quick fix theory, people have come to think that the answer to all ailments can be found in the utilization of a drug or a chemical. Rather than looking for the cause of health, science has been concentrating on trying to find the cause of disease and on defining the ability to fight this disease. As a population we have spent too much time focusing on sickness and disease, when it has become apparent that the focus must shift to health and well-being. Based on the appreciation of life itself, it is sound to reason that health comes from the inside out and not from the outside in. Healing must, therefore, take place from an internal environment within man/woman and cannot be introduced from the outside. We recognize that life itself is a constructive force that maintains health, and it is your job to maintain that function at its optimum.

When was the last time you looked at a newborn baby and appreciated this child for more than it's outside physical appearance and beauty? When was the last time you realized the total perfection and total health of a newborn baby, recognizing that 40 weeks prior, two cells came together and after multiple divisions, formed a beautiful child. How is it that these cells knew exactly what to become and where to go, and how to function when they came together? How is it that all this cellular information does not end in chaos, but rather ends up in an intelligent form called a human being? It is not conceivable through logical reasoning, that this human being, so intelligently created, must inherently possess the very intelligence to maintain itself in a state of health, is it?

What we know to be true is that all bodily functions in a human being are under the direction of the nervous system. The messages that originate in the brain, controlling all human bodily functions, travel down the spinal cord and branch out to give energy and life force to every single tissue, in every single cell, in the wonderful apparatus called a human being. This nerve energy, when uninterrupted, allows every cell, tissue and every organ, to function in harmony with the total being. Recognizing the very importance of the central nervous system, being the master control system of the human body, nature and her wisdom has protected the brain within a solid skull, and the spinal cord within the bony masses of the spinal column called vertebrae. Openings between the vertebrae become passageways for the nerves to exit and enter, bringing all energy to and from all tissues of the human body. This network forms a communication system from the brain, down the spinal cord, through the spinal nerves to all organs and tissue cells of the human body, as well as from the cells back to the brain. In order for the human body to function, communication must exist continuously between the brain and all structures, and then from the structures back to the brain.

If interference occurs along the pathway of this communication system, the end tissue cell will be deprived of its required neurological energy, and will consequently malfunction. Interference usually occurs as the nerves course between vertebrae, and in chiropractic this state is referred to as a subluxation. Why do I share this information with you? Science has proven that the nervous system governs all functions of the human body, and when interference occurs it is impossible for you to function at your optimum. Now that you know, make it your responsibility to attend a chiropractor's office and have your spine and nervous system checked for subluxation. I urge you to also do the same for your loved ones. We recognize that a healthy diet, regular exercise and proper sleep are necessities for optimal health and a truly vibrant life. Not one of these alone will make you healthy, and without optimal nervous system function, optimal health is never achieved. Chiropractic is a necessary and safe form of health care for everyone. Every person, from the newborn to those living their golden years, is better off without nervous system interference.

You may be asking how do chiropractors correct these subluxations? Chiropractors through a very rigorous course of study are trained to detect and correct spinal subluxations via the chiropractic adjustment. Adjustments serve one purpose, the correction of vertebral subluxations to enhance function of the nervous system. By doing so, body systems usually function at their optimum and consequently signs and symptoms, the warning signs of dysfunction, are alleviated. You may often hear chiropractic patients state:"My chiropractor cured my asthma, my headaches, my digestion, etc." In fact it is important to recognize that chiropractic and the chiropractor do not claim to heal or cure any condition. The purpose of chiropractic is to enhance spinal function, clearing the communication channels of the nervous system, leading to overall improved body function.

What you can expect following spinal correction when necessary, is an improved sense of well-being. Some individuals experience immediate benefits following the adjustment, others with more severe subluxations experience a return to health over time. As a rule, spinal adjustments are not painful, though some patients report experiencing mild discomfort following the first few adjustments. This apparent negative sensation usually subsides with a few adjustments and is attributed to physiological changes of the body tissues. Spinal correction takes time: weeks, months or years for some people. In time, most people receiving adjustments will describe a sense of relaxation, well-being and peace. No wonder people who undergo corrective chiropractic care always want to continue with their adjustments. Why wouldn't they, when chiropractic adjustments offer so many benefits for total health? The euphoria described by many appears to be due to the freeing of nerve energy, flowing from above down. This is restoration of health, restoration of life.

Everyone can benefit from chiropractic care. How long you decide to benefit from chiropractic care remains a personal decision for every single individual.

Scientific research is proving the direct relationship between the nervous system and the immune system. The immune system governs whether or not people fall victim to infectious or other detrimental processes. Since the nervous system controls all functions and healing in the human body, and can be put in jeopardy by spinal dysfunction, it is imperative that everyone have optimal spinal and nervous system function. No doctor in the world, with any amount of drugs or technology, could possibly duplicate the magnificence and wonder of the human body: a wisdom that not only runs every intricate detail of its function, but also has a built-in safeguard to fight disease. It is imperative to allow the free expression of this wisdom, remove any interference to the nervous system, free the body of subluxations via the adjustment, and allow the human being to live its optimal life.

"The natural healing force is the greatest healing force in getting man well."

- Hippocrates

Please remember that symptoms are the last stages of malfunction, not the first. By the time symptoms have occurred, years of opportunity for correction and repair have been lost. Would it not be wise to correct vertebral subluxations when they occur, rather than wait years for damage to take place and symptoms to take over your body? Have your spine and nervous system examined today. Get on a program to correct your spinal subluxations if necessary, and join the millions of people who've taken responsibility for their health and receive regular chiropractic care. If you want to achieve and maintain optimum health, make chiropractic part of your life for life. It has been said by many that regular chiropractic care saves lives, adds life to years and years to your life. Invest in a correction and prevention program, reap the rewards and give the gift of great health to your loved ones.

"While other professions are concerned with changing the environment to suit the weakened body, chiropractic is concerned with strengthening the body to suit the environment.'

- B.J.Palmer DC

Many political leaders call the present universal disease care system a healthcare system, based on the mistaken belief that the best way to help health is to spend even more money fighting disease. In actual fact, health is a natural state of the body, and sickness and disease are abnormal conditions that can often be corrected by the body's own inborn intelligence. Chiropractors promote a natural approach to achieving and maintaining good health. We believe that drugs or surgery should be used only after all options have been exhausted or when a patient's life is being threatened.

Throughout the years, the efforts of chiropractors have helped millions achieve a better level of health, and today, chiropractic continues to expand and flourish as the third-largest primary healthcare profession in the world. Now that you know, what different decision will you make to achieve optimal health?

"I believe that to meet the challenges of our times, human beings will have to develop a greater sense of universal responsibility. Each of us must learn to work not just for oneself, one's own family or nation, but for the benefit of all humankind. Universal responsibility is the key to human survival. It is the best foundation for world peace."

His Holiness the Dalai Lama

Chapter Four

Social Responsibility –
Making a difference in the life of others

My favorite quote as it relates to social responsibility is by former President of the United States, John Fitzgerald Kennedy. I recall clearly hearing him say this on television decades ago and it has been repeated so many times by so many.

"Ask not what your country can do for you - ask what you can do for your country."

We could choose to paraphrase this quote and have it read "ask not what others can do for you - ask what you can do for others." If we chose to live life from this particular perspective how different would society be, how different would your life experiences be? Margaret Thatcher former Prime Minister of Britain said: "We want a society in which we are free to make choices, to make mistakes, to be generous and compassionate. That is what we mean by a moral society - not a society which the State is responsible for everything, and no one is responsible for the State." This is also a very profound statement. Though we enjoy the fruits of labor of our forefathers it is imperative to recognize that freedom is not free. Freedom requires a keen sense of citizen responsibility if it is to be maintained, and if it is to flourish and survive. The course of history has been changed by many men and women willing to take responsibility, willing to dare. Life is an exhilarating adventure, and it can also be a struggle. Every great success ever achieved in history was achieved by those who took responsibility and had the courage to dare. The men or women who dare court hardship, do so because they see the possibility of participating in creating a better world. They have no time for doubt. They make the impossible - possible. They recognize that failure is not final or fatal. And not to make the attempt, that is the unredeemable failure. The courage to dare, the courage to take responsibility for what could be provides force and fortitude. The world definitely seeks those who are willing to throw themselves into the battle; those who take a position unconventional. For many people, responsibility appears to have taken a backseat. It is time for society to give heart and spirit to any fear or terror, reclaim the world of possibility and take action. Unless you've been completely cut off from communication networks since the mid two thousands, you're likely aware of the problems that have plagued the global economy, and have affected countless individuals and nations. As ridiculous as this may sound, these problems stem from the impact of social icons as much as they stem from those in the political arena. No we are not in this predicament solely because of terrorism or bureaucrats. We're here because we have become a population that rebels against virtue and character, and chooses instead to value the emptiness of fame and fortune. Unfortunately, relying on fame and/or fortune for happiness presents a ground for disaster. Just ask anyone who has ever been rich or famous. Read the stories of athletes, actors, .com millionaires, who have fallen out of favor. They recognize that their focus on fame and fortune, and away from virtue and responsibility, has been their nemesis.

I read a story recently in an e-mail and though I cannot quote its source, the story provides great value as it relates to social responsibility.

"While attending a recent homeowner's association meeting, my wife and I were overwhelmed by the attitude of the majority of our neighbors. With few exceptions, they wanted everything done for them and thought all they had do was sit around and complain loudly enough to make it happen. After about 15 minutes of complaints and finger-pointing, I chimed in on a specific issue with, "What if each of us committed to doing our part to help make things better for everyone?" The crowd fell silent for a good 5 seconds (which felt like eternity in a room full of 50 people), before everyone astoundingly agreed. I don't think that my neighbors were incapable of thinking up such a simple solution on their own. Rather, I think this is an illustration of the depth of their cultural dependence and reliance on others for seemingly everything in life."

Too many people walk around thinking "Who can I blame?" rather than saying "How can I contribute?" Imagine how much better life would be if people chose to focus on how they can individually contribute to the greater good of society.

"When it's all over, it's not who you were... it's whether you made a difference."

Bob Doyle

If you are committed to being a contributor, to being responsible for the world in which we live, it is imperative that you become aware of your internal language and the language you communicate to others. Sam Narisi wrote an article entitled *Five worst words to say at work*. It is suggested that as you develop awareness for the words utilized, you will be able to stop yourself before saying any of the five statements that are described below.

1) "I'll try." Your intentions may be noble, but this statement is noncommittal, and does not speak of responsibility or accountability.

2) "I'll get back to you." For most this sounds like a stalling tactic. Instead choose to specify a time when you will get back to the person, and maintain a high level of accountability to follow through. Example: "I will get back with you tomorrow by 10:00am."

3) "We'll see." Most people who utilize this statement want to either avoid confrontation or avoid saying no. Choose to be responsible for your answers and be honest.

4) "I guess ..." This phrase gives people the impression that you really do not know what you're talking about and that you are not willing to take responsibility for the outcome. If you're ready to take a position, state it and follow through. If you are <u>not</u> ready to make a decision state that as well.

5) "If." For example, "If my assistant completes what I asked her to do, then I will be able to do my part." Choose to assume a successful outcome and speak in terms of "when" rather than terms of "if".

On the next few pages I will share stories that should enhance your vision of responsibility.

After You Make the Wrong Call

Some mistakes are memorable not because they provide pyrotechnics but because they show character.

Case in Point: During the summer of 2010 major league umpire Jim Joyce made the most important call of his career and it was wrong. His mistake cost Detroit's 28-year-old pitcher Armando Galarraga a perfect game. Only 20 times in major league history has the pitcher turned away 27 straight batters - three up, three down in nine innings. After reviewing the video, Joyce immediately admitted that he'd blown the call. He went straight to the clubhouse to apologize. Galarraga told him to forget about it, saying nobody's perfect. Later, the pitcher said he felt worse for the ump than he did for himself. Both men, observes The Wall Street Journal speech writer and columnist Peggy Noonan, "comported themselves as fully formed adults, with patience, grace and dignity," the pitcher showing empathy, and the umpire, as a figure of authority, freely admitting his mistake, with no attempt to spin his decision or dig in his heels.

"I just cost the kid a perfect game", he announced, clearly shaken. "I was convinced he beat the throw until I saw the replay. It was the biggest call of my career."

That kind of maturity is rare. Too many in our society don't know how to accept responsibility for their errors and therefore are unable to pass on this skill to the next generation. There presently exists a huge mentoring gap between this present generation and the previous generation. As we become more aware of the entitlement issue, and recognize that this is not serving our children, what will we do to make the change? When it is said that the current generation is predicted to not outlive their parents, due to inappropriate health choices, it has become obvious that developing and mastering the art of responsibility is no longer an option. We must lead with courage, insight, vitality and vigor.

Leading the charge may not be easy, but it has become necessary. During the month of August 2010, I read an article in The Business Management Daily publication Executive Leadership, entitled *Leadership on the High Seas*. I share it with you below.

On the Maersk Alabama, a U.S. - flagged cargo ship, the captain's cool head, long experience, clear sense of duty -along with some luck- saved the ship from Pirates off Africa's east coast. "It never ends like this," says Richard Phillips. The captain gave himself ashostage and spent five days after in a lifeboat before his rescue by Navy SEALs. To understand why it did end so well for Phillips and his crew, you have to go back to his days as a seaman learning by example that deeds count, not words. That respect counts, not yelling. That you never show fear. …. Capt. Phillips says, "I felt that if you did the job right, if you let people be themselves and crack down only when they blew an assignment, then morale would take care of itself. You have to show people that you deserve the respect that goes along with the title Capt. You can't browbeat them into looking up to you." Phillips acknowledged that he's tough to work for, and he takes his responsibility for his men and ship very seriously. He trains his men relentlessly to handle worst-case scenarios. One of his hardest workers gave Phillips the best complement ever. "You know, you are a pain in the ass, but I know what you're going to say before you say it", meaning he's consistent. And the key to Capt. Phillips leadership skills is based on his motto: "we are all here for the ship. The ship isn't here for us." And there was an unspoken part of that saying that he kept to himself: "the Capt. is here for the crew." That the captain comes last isn't just a line in a movie, Phillips says: "It's my duty".

Such is the level of duty and responsibility that we must bring to the forefront. Being individually responsible and accountable for social justice, personal and business relationships, our communities, our families, and our environment, will encourage others to do the same. Let's all choose to be the change we wish to see in the world, and the change will take place. Of that I am convinced. It's time to give people hope. I am not talking about simply creating a feeling of expectation and desire for certain things to happen, or a belief that something good may happen. What I am asking is that you believe in yourself and those around you, because thousands of people succeeded despite the odds against them, and you could too. This is legitimate grounds for hope. Hope energizes dreams and fuels possibilities. It is not a promise. It is an invitation. There is never a good reason not to hope, never a good reason not to choose responsibility.

"Don't spend your precious time asking 'Why isn't the world a better place? ' It will only be time wasted. The question to ask is 'How can I make it better? 'To that there is an answer."

Leo F. Buscaglia

Chapter Five –

Supportive Quotes

This chapter is filled with quotes from famous and some not so famous individuals who spoke on the issue of responsibility. Some of these people you have certainly heard of, some you may have no idea about. It really doesn't matter. It's the wisdom in the words that matters. You may ask "why so many?" After all, you have read this book and certainly have an understanding of the importance of responsibility. I chose these quotes and ask you to read one at a time. Take time in between each to understand what this quote could mean in your life; what change you may be willing to make because of these words of wisdom. Such introspection can lead to an improved self or social condition. The discovery could give you wings to become better at your profession or at parenting. Countless people may be positively affected because you chose to read this book. Read with the intent to truly understand and you will make a tremendous difference in the lives of many.

"The price of greatness is responsibility."

– Sir Winston Churchill

"Man must cease attributing his problems to his environment, and learn again to exercise his will – his personal responsibility."

\- Albert Einstein

"It is easy to dodge our responsibilities, but we cannot judge the consequences of dodging our responsibilities."

– Josiah Charles Stamp

"You are not only responsible for what you say; you are also responsible for what you don't say."

– Martin Luther King

"Let everyone sweep in front of his own door, and the world will be clean."

– Johann Wolfgang von Goethe

"Be the change you want to see in the world."

– Mahatma Gandhi

"Life is a gift, and it offers us the privilege, opportunity, and responsibility to give something back by becoming more."

– Anthony Robbins

"Today more than ever before, life must be characterized by a sense of Universal responsibility, not only nation to nation and human to human, but also human to other forms of life."

— The Dalai Lama

"I never look at the masses as my responsibility; I look at the individual. I can only love one person at a time — just one, one, one. So you begin. I began — I picked up one person. Maybe if I didn't pick up that one person, I wouldn't have picked up forty-two thousand... the same thing goes for you, the same thing in your family, the same thing in your church, your community. Just begin — one, one, one."

— Mother Teresa of Calcutta

"Freedom is the will to be responsible to ourselves."

— Friedrich Nietzsche

"It is the responsibility of leadership to provide opportunity, and the responsibility of individuals to contribute."

— William Pollard

"We are alone with no excuses. That is the idea I shall try to convey when I say that man is condemned to be free. Condemned because he did not create himself, yet, in other respects is free; because once thrown into the world, he is responsible for everything he does".

— Jean Paul Sartre

"We have the Bill of Rights. What we need is a Bill of Responsibilities."

— Bill Maher

"Nothing strengthens the judgment and quickens the conscience like individual responsibility."

-Elizabeth Cady Stanton

"I believe that every right implies a responsibility; every opportunity, an obligation; every possession a duty."

-John D. Rockefeller

"You cannot escape the responsibility of tomorrow by evading it today."

-Abraham Lincoln

"Hold yourself responsible for a higher standard than anybody else expects of you. Never excuse yourself. Never pity yourself. Be a hard master to yourself – and be lenient to everybody else."

- Henry Ward Beecher

"I will not surrender responsibility for my life and my actions."

- John Enoch Powell

"When we have begun to take charge of our lives, to own ourselves, there is no longer any need to ask permission of someone."

- George O'Neil

"No alibi will save you from accepting responsibility."

- Napoleon Hill

"Accept responsibility for your life. Know that it is you who will get you to where you want to go, no one else."

- Les Brown

"Within each of us lies the power of our consent to health and sickness, to riches and poverty, to freedom and slavery. It is we who control these and not another."

\- Richard Bach

"A sense of wisdom and maturity is when you come to terms with the realization that your decisions cause you rewards and consequences. You are responsible for your life, and your ultimate success depends on the choices you make."

\- Dennis Waitley

"You must take personal responsibility. You cannot change the circumstances, the season, or the wind, but you can change yourself. That is something you have charge of."

\- Jim Rohn

"Whatever happens, take responsibility."

\- Anthony Robbins

"Put all excuses aside, and remember that you are capable of taking responsibility."

\- Gilles LaMarche

"Each is responsible for his own actions."

- H.L. Hunt

"Refuse to be average. Let your heart soar as high as it will."

- A.W. Tozer

"The willingness to accept responsibility for one's own life is the source form which self-respect springs."

- Joan Didion

"Action springs not from thought, but from a readiness for responsibility."

- Dietrich Bonhoeffer

"Responsibility walks hand in hand with capacity and power."

- Josiah Gilbert Holland

"In dreams begin responsibility."

- William Butler Yates

"Responsibilities gravitate to the person who can shoulder them."

- Tom Stoppard

"Man must cease attributing his problems to this environment, and learn again to exercise his will – his responsibility."

- Albert Schweitzer

"The best job goes to the person who can get it done without passing the buck or coming back with excuses."

- Napoleon Hill

"If you don't run your own life, someone else will."

- John Atkinson

"Each player must accept the cards that life deals him or her. But once in hand one must decide how to play the cards in order to win the game."

- Voltaire

Take Action Now

AFFIRMATION for GROWTH – "I choose to read quotes that support my personal development."

- Pick a topic or a series of topics that you wish to expand/improve in your life
- Search for quotes that relate to that topic
- Choose the ones that are best suited to you, and some that may stretch your thinking process
- Write these quotes and keep each series of quote topics on a separate sheet
- Choose to read these quotes daily for at least 21 days, and reflect on each for a few moments
- You will discover a new awareness

For example if you want to improve your responsibility towards expressing your love for the people in your life, search for quotes on love, make a list as below and read them daily. You will soon have a new understanding and appreciation for the value of communicating love.

Love Quotes

Love is always bestowed as a gift – freely, willingly and without expectation. We don't love to be loved; we love to love.

- Leo Buscaglia

Love is like a roller coaster,
Once you have completed the ride,
you want to go again.

- Unknown

Love is the only way to grasp another human being in the innermost core of his personality.

- Viktor E. Frankl

Love is sweet when it's new, but sweeter when it's true.
Love is like a butterfly, it settles upon you when you least expect it.
Love is the hardest habit to break, and the most difficult to satisfy.

- Drew Barrymore

Remember that great love and great achievements involve great risk.

- Anonymous

Forever is not a word…rather a place where two lovers go when true love takes them there.

- Unknown

Where the sacred laws of honor are once invaded, love makes the easier conquest.

- Addison

Ancient lovers believed a kiss would literally unite their souls, because the spirit was said to be carried in one's breath.

- Eve Glicksman

Not all of us have to possess earthshaking talent. Just common sense and love will do.

- Myrtle Auvil

When they asked me what I loved most about life, I smiled and said you.

- Unknown

I have learned not to worry about love;
But to honor its coming with all my heart.

- Alice Walker

I speak in hugs & kisses because true love never misses. I will lead
or follow to be with you tomorrow.

- Unknown

One does not fall "in" or "out" of love. One grows in love.

- Leo Buscaglia

Love appears in moments, how long can I hold a moment, as my
moment fades, I yearn to catch sight or sound of you, to feel the
surging of my heart erupt into joyous sounds of laughter.

- Chris Watson

Within you, I lose myself. Without you,
I find myself wanting to be lost again.

- Unknown

Love is the only satisfactory answer to the problem of human
existence.

- Erich Fromm

Love gives light even in the darkest tunnel.

- Anonymous

Love is always within. When you try to dramatize your love, you lose the depth of the love.

- Charan Singh

To love is to admire with the heart: to admire is to love with the mind.

- Theophile Gautier

If you love someone you would be willing to give up everything for them, but if they loved you back they'd never ask you to.

- Anon

Love, like a mountain-wind upon an oak, falling upon me, shakes me leaf and bough.

- Sappho

If love is a game, it has to be the hardest game in the world. After all, how can anyone win a game where there are no rules?

- Cody Meyers

If you have love in your life it can make up for a great many things you lack. If you don't have it, no matter what else there is, it's not enough.

- Ann Landers

When it comes to unconditional love, Saint Francis of Assisi appears to have said it best:

Make me an instrument of your peace.
Where there is hatred, let me sow love;
Where there is injury, pardon;
Where there is doubt, faith;
Where there is despair, hope;
Where there is darkness, light;
Where there is sadness, joy.
Grant that I may not so much seek to be consoled, as to console;
To be understood, as to understand;
To be loved as to love.
For it is in giving that we receive;
It is in pardoning that we are pardoned;
And it is in dying that we are born to eternal life.

May you find the value in choosing responsibility to create the life that you want to live; one where you utilize your gifts, talents, qualities and attributes to serve those around you. Always remember that life is about service, and that "service is the rent you pay for taking up space on this wonderful planet."

Chapter Six –

The Power of Affirmations to support your growth

An Affirmation is a declaration that something is true. Affirmations are statements of fact.

Every thought you think and every word you say is an affirmation. Even your self-talk is a stream of affirmations, whether supportive or destructive. You are continually affirming subconsciously with your words and thoughts. This flow of affirmations is creating your life experience in every moment. Your beliefs are learned thought patterns that have developed since childhood. Many of these thoughts work well for you, but others may now be working against you. Some may even be sabotaging you from achieving what you want.

Your subconscious uses the behavior patterns you have learned to automatically respond and react to everyday events. Your learned responses and thought patterns enable you to automatically respond to circumstances quickly and easily. Problems arise however, if at an early stage some of the foundation beliefs on which many others are built were formed from a skewed perspective. Often such beliefs are inappropriate for succeeding in the real world.

You can use appropriate statements derived from your chosen thoughts to target and improve specific subconscious beliefs. These statements will also remove the negative beliefs that have been undermining your life success and freedom. Some may tell you that this is a form of "brainwashing", and maybe it is. But it is you choosing the thoughts that you allow in, and which negative beliefs to wash away. The way these statements are constructed is extremely important, a process we will share shortly.

Do affirmations work?

YES! Affirmations really work, and here's why?

Neuroscience has shown us that repeated thoughts create synaptic connections in your brain that lead to behavior and form your character. Your life experiences create these cell to cell, neuron to neuron connections like branches on a tree. Every time you are faced with a similar situation, you react or respond in a similar fashion, until you choose to repeatedly change the thought processes and create new connections. There is good news. As you create new connections and stop using the "old patterns" that have previously ruled your life, the old patterns break down, and so do the connections in your brain. This process is called "pruning", as if you were pruning branches from a tree. Choosing healthier, happier and more positive thoughts lead you to living the life you want. Measurable physiological changes in your brain chemistry take place and morphological changes in the connections within your brain are seen.

By choosing to think in terms of what you want to be, do or have in your life, and saying positive affirmations as true, your subconscious mind is forced into one of two reactions - avoidance or reappraisal. The bigger the issue, the bigger the gap between the positive affirmation and the perceived inner truth, and the more likely you are going to experience resistance. This is where the subconscious finds it easier to stay with its perceived inner truth and avoid the challenge using any means at its disposal to avoid examining the issue. You will recognize this reaction by a strong negative feeling inside as you state the positive affirmations; often one of "Right, that's not possible. That's not who I am. I can't be that or do that." Equally, if you experience a sense of joy and well being, your mind is instinctively responding to something it believes to be true. When you experience this emotion, you know your affirmations are working!

Continually repeating affirmations with conviction and passion will chip away at even the strongest resistance. Once the resistance is broken, your subconscious is able to re-examine the core beliefs and patterns you have been working on. The effect can be startling and things can change very quickly as the dysfunctional beliefs get identified and replaced by your own new inner truth. Depending on how deep into your consciousness these beliefs lay, every other learned pattern and belief that relied on the original belief as a premise, becomes unfounded. The subconscious has to re-examine them all, this can lead to a period of introspection. Consider this period in your life as a great voyage, one where you will have the capacity to evaluate your core values and choose those that support your life plan.

Because affirmations actually reprogram your thought patterns, they change the way you think and feel about things. Because you have replaced dysfunctional beliefs with your own new positive beliefs, positive change comes more easily and naturally.

How quickly do affirmations work?

From day one, there will be affirmations you love and enjoy saying. These affirmations are likely to be very effective for you and you are likely to start experiencing changes almost immediately. Others will feel very negative, almost like a big lie. This indicates resistance, and these areas may take longer to impact. How quickly you can resolve such an issue is like asking how long a piece of string is. It depends on the issue; how deeply the belief is held and how determined you are to bring about change in that area of your life. If you are truly ready and want to make changes, the quicker those changes will occur. People have made cognitive changes in their beliefs almost instantaneously. Once you are prepared to embrace and accept a change, and you believe it to be right for you, that change will happen. So it is not really a question of time, more a question of how accepting of change you choose to be.

Will Affirmations help me?

Yes. No matter who you are or what aspect of life you're dealing with, affirmations will make you feel better about yourself and your life. When used correctly, they can manifest real change in your life. Changing the way you think, reprogramming your mind and removing the old negative beliefs that have been sabotaging you again and again, affirmations can enable you to achieve the life you aspire living. The main objective is to do the things needed to acquire the attitudes and characteristics of the person who would, as a natural outcome, be the person you want to become and have the things you want to have in your life. This is where you will focus your energy in the present, fully engaged in the process.

Turning dreams into reality takes goal directed action. You cannot wish hard enough, fantasize long enough, or pour your intentions into the ether powerfully enough to simply manifest your dreams. As you focus your energy on accomplishing your goals by faithfully reciting your chosen affirmations, you are likely to experience a wonderful surprise - the Universe opening doors of opportunity.

How do I write an affirmation?

When you have identified an area of your life that you want to improve write an affirmation as if you had already achieved what you want, who you choose to become, how you choose to behave. An affirmation must be spoken in the first person starting with the declaration "I am" or other specific declaration of "I". An affirmation should contain adjectives that stir positive emotions deep within you. Below I share a number of affirmations that I have used over the years, something I continue daily more than three decades later.

- I choose to be enthusiastically responsible
- I am focused on the task of today
- I am self-directed and choose to write my affirmations
- I am talented and capable of accomplishing this task with excellence
- I always do the work that a failure will not do
- I choose to let my reach exceed my grasp
- I raise my goals as soon as they are attained
- I always strive to make the next hour better than this one
- I am worth my weight in precious gold

- I am exquisite and worthy of love, kindness and respect
- I am worthy because I exist
- I am worthy of the best that life has to offer
- I am joyfully confident in my ability to make my life work
- I choose exceptional health, healing and happiness
- I trust with certainty that my highest good and greatest joy are unfolding before me
- I live in the light of my higher mind and allow it to illuminate my wonderful journey
- I am divinely worthy of receiving God's revelations and gifts.
- I am unconditional love to the world
- I am a master of persistence and I do whatever it takes
- I am peaceful and quiet, and listen to my heart's song
- I am unconditional love, I am peace, I am a shining brilliant light
- I follow my heart's deepest desire for truth and goodness
- I look for exquisite joy in myself and see joy in the world that surrounds me
- I delight and share joy with others
- I enthusiastically let my heart shine and give from the depths of my being to those who accept love
- I joyously count my blessings daily
- I intently listen to the truth of others, and I share my truth honestly
- I develop exceptional strength every time I meet a life challenge

- I trust the serene wisdom of my inner voice.
- I express my love and goodness each time I speak
- I open myself to know my inner guidance and deepest wisdom
- I am unlimited in my capacity for joy, healing and happiness
- I release and forgive myself and others for all past transgressions
- I live in the light of my truth and I accept what I know to be true
- I am happily filled by God's grace, light and love
- I create clarity of mind and unlimited vision for myself
- I trust that my highest good and greatest joy are unfolding
- I am wise, intuitive, and align with my highest good
- I seek wisdom and guidance in all situations
- I open my creative imagination to see the very best in people, and I also see the best in myself
- I know with certainty that all is well in my world
- I enthusiastically honor everyone I interact with
- I respectfully honor my body and treat myself and others with respect
- I trust my feelings and give them ample room for full expression
- I receive pleasure and abundance with every exquisite breath I take
- I rest, relax, and enjoy myself knowing that healing takes place
- I enthusiastically stimulate my immunity by knowing that God lives in and through me

- I incur healing each time I affirm my worth and honor my choices for love
- I love who I am, exactly as I am
- I know I am a powerful and wholesome force for good
- I find extreme joy, fulfillment, and value in the way I invest my life
- I am present in the here and now
- I find personal satisfaction, joy and fulfillment in all the roles I play
- I have a realistic understanding of the relationship between who I am, what I do, the contributions I make, and the rewards and benefits I receive
- I realistically allocate my time and energy between multiple roles to maximize my efficiency
- I am effective, efficient, and accountable
- I effectively manage the gap between who I am and who I want to become
- I effectively manage the gap between what I have and what I want
- I function well in stressful situations without being distracted or having the need to complain, place blame or make excuses
- I invest energy in doing things that are important, and that add value to my life and the life of others
- I consistently look for the good in others, and when I see it, I share it
- I choose to be real, genuine and authentic

Now choose to write affirmations that will bring you closer to living the life you are worthy of living. That's the life you dream about, the one you aspire living, that until now you have not taken responsibility to create. Your past is past. Your future is a clean slate and you are the artist who can choose to paint what you want on that blank canvas. Happy travels as you step into your world and experience **The ART of Responsibility –freedom to create your life.**

After reading this book I suspect that you are willing to utilize the invisible yet knowable life force within you to create a better life. If you are presently in desperation, realize that this is simply a smokescreen of bigger and better days ahead. The road which follows is that of the stronger man or woman who sooner or later says "I can". When you become passionate about your life and your capacity to contribute, you recognize that it is not necessary to throw up your hands in despair. You can choose a little more effort and a little more patience, and what seemed hopeless failure will usually turn into glorious success.

"In the confrontation between the stream and the rock, the stream always wins ... not through strength but by perseverance."

- H. Jackson Brown

You are now ready to take concerted action responsibly.

Take Action Now

Focus on who you want to become. Who is this person? What characteristics or attributes does this person have?

_____

_____

_____

_____

_____

_____

_____

_____

_____

_____

_____

_____

_____

_____

_____

_____

AFFIRMATION for GROWTH – *I create my plan and work my plan*

- Choose to improve yourself daily.
- Decide and write down who you want to become, the person who would, as a natural outcome, achieve what you want to achieve.
- Decide what you want to have in your life. These are your dreams.
- Identify the attributes and characteristics of the person you want to become.
- Identify the actions required to acquire these characteristics or attributes.

- Create the affirmations that will support you on this journey.

You can focus strictly on having what you want, or you can focus on taking the actions needed to become the person who will ultimately have what you want. The first approach is driven by expectations, often unrealistic, and the second is driven by reality - action filled purposeful life, living in the here and now. The differences you will experience are like day and night - frustration versus joy, hope versus fear, peace versus resentment, fulfillment versus anxiety. Yes, this will require that you take complete responsibility for your thoughts and your actions, thereby creating the feelings you want to experience most of the time, and living a life that until now you only dreamt possible.

"I will persist until I succeed."

"Always remember: with awareness comes responsibility – responsibility to act and BE who you want to be, achieving what you want to achieve; leaving the legacy you want to create."

- Gilles LaMarche

Follow the three R's:

- *Respect for self*
- *Respect for others*
- *Responsibility for all your actions*

About the Author

Gilles' lifelong quest for continuous improvement lead him to study psychology and the philosophy of success for more than 30 years. He has spoken to audiences throughout Canada, USA, Mexico, Europe, the UK, Australia, Japan and the Bahamas. He is the author and co-author of 11 books, including "Steering Your Ship Called Life", "The Sports Injuries Symposium",, "Wake up – Live the Life you Love" , "Say YES to Chiropractic Success" , "Tired of Being Sick and Tired", "The Well Adjusted Soul", and "The ART of Responsibility", all highly acclaimed by readers.

He is a professional speaker, writer, and business/personal development coach to a number of professionals and executives. He was chosen to appear in The National Registry's Who's Who in Executives and Professionals 2001-2002 edition. He has been involved in sports as an athlete since childhood. He still runs and works out regularly to maintain a high level of physical and mental fitness.

Gilles has learned to balance his life, enjoying a successful professional career and a wonderful personal life. He is a passionate spokesperson encouraging people to take responsibility for the gift of health.

His personal philosophy encompasses mind, body and spirit. He believes in the great importance of commitment and responsibility to the world in which we live. He is a doctor, a teacher, a friend, and most importantly Dad to three terrific young adults. His mission: to help all those he meets achieve their potential. He has pledged his life to his greatest expression of love and service for the benefit of humanity. Gilles is a little man with a big heart and open spirit, an inspiration to all who seek to better themselves and discover their true potential.

To book Dr. LaMarche to speak at your next conference you may contact him via email at gilles@gilleslamarche.com or by telephone at 214-282-1500.

You may purchase additional copies of The ART of Responsibility at www.parkershareproducts.com or on Amazon